read(writ)ing

Published by Penteract Press, 2020

PenteractPress.com
PenteractPress@gmail.com
Twitter.com/PenteractPress

Designed by Rachel Smith

rachelartsmith.com
twitter: @rachelartsmith
instagram: rachel_artsmith

Typeset in Baskerville

FIRST EDITION

ISBN 978-1-913421-04-5

read(writ)ing *words*

A Meandering Material Dialogue

Rachel Smith

with

HMRCollective

Many thanks are due to Helen Frank and Madeleine Walton for their enthusiasm and generosity of spirit throughout this project.

erfectly symbolized his audacity, he refused the Nobel Prize for iterature in 1964. Fired by a passion for freedom and justice, loved and ated in his own day, Sartre stands as the authentic modern successor to oltaire, Victor Hugo and Émile Zola.

PROLOGUE

*

READING

look

identify

lift

Reading Jean Paul Sartre's childhood autobiography I am drawn to the dividing sections: Reading and Writing. Struck by this seperation, associations gather. Simultaneously I read Roland Barthes as he outlines a system of writing his reading process. Ideas spark an exploration of reading, writing, and making, and my experience of their entangled relation, as a read(writ)ing method.

skim

trigger

narrow

'the reader is the very space
in which are inscribed, [...] all citations out of which a writing is made'.

'A real reader is a writer'.

'a good reader, a major reader, an active and creative reader is a re-reader.

'the ideal reader, unlike the contemporary reader, is a purely fictional being'
yet the contemporary reader
'is difficult to mould to the form of a generalisation'

'A different world (the reader's) slips into the authors place'

reading as renting:
'Renters make comparable changes in an apartment they furnish with their acts and memories; as do speakers, in language'

'reading as poaching'

'the reader cannot protect [her]self against the erosion of time'

To admit authorities, [...]
into our libraries
and let them tell us how to read,
what to read [...]
is to destroy the spirit of freedom which is the breath of those sanctuaries'

concentrate

search

choose

Reading concentration
interrupted

tracing the drift across the page

the event of reading is more difficult to analyse than the separate elements of text and reader

adapt methods of operating in-amongst

reading as a searching action

skimming the surface to narrow down a selection

glancing to identify fragments

lifting

inhabiting the space in-amongst provokes a sense of lostness but enables a tracing of any routes performed

the reader reaches towards the writer

gathering associations

re-turning as the earthworm

bookworm

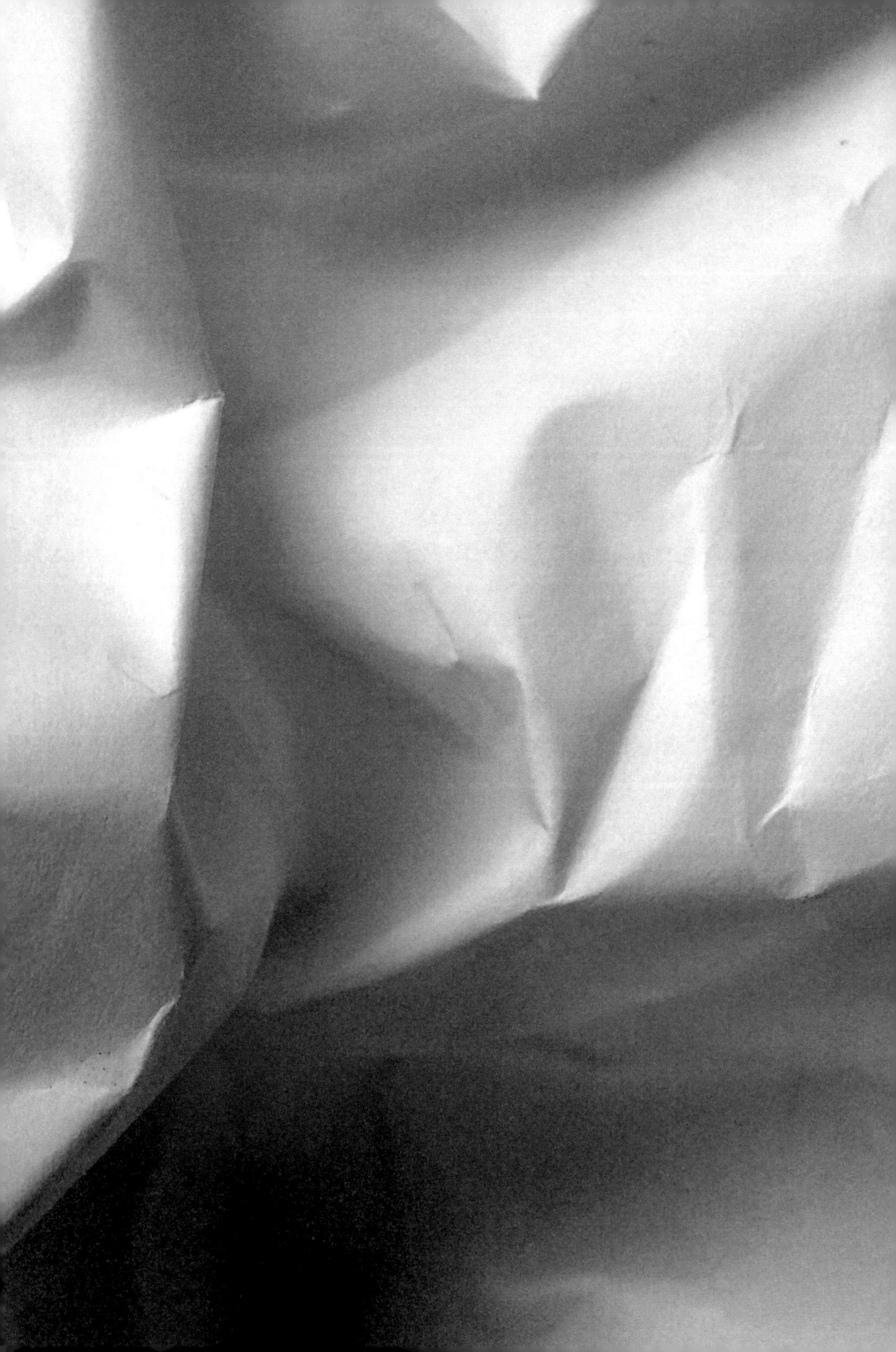

READ(WRIT)ING

*

read(writ)ing is the term I have developed to explore the synthesis of *reading as writing as making*, using processes of drawing, photography, and writing. As an activity it occupies the speculative position of being in-amongst so as to avoid static or oppositional positions in language, entangling any meanings that may arise.

generate

question

synthesise

It is arduous to separate the productive activities of reading, writing, and making. Reading frequently involves doodling, tangential distractions, note taking, or mentally constructing ideas all of which begin the blurring of any boundaries. Writing is soaked in phrases from previous and concurrent reading. Making is a material production of the thoughts while reading or writing. The visible process in these pages is a collaborative activity, as sense is collectively sought. The assemblage of fragments explores how sense might be de-con-structed, developing a generative method as an amalgamation of theory and practice.

I have been impersonating a reader; copying the behaviour of a reader so well that anyone who cared to notice would think that I have read Les Mots

anyone who cared to notice would think that I have read Les Mots

mpersonating
nirror performance
ehaviour copied
no-one is watching you read

assume
the position
a *life* spent *turning around by repeating the same moves*
coming and going rather than starting and finishing

I don't impersonate a reader.
I don't copy the behaviour of a reader.
I am a reader.

splintered moments

associations mobilised in-amongst assembled remnants

drawing-out-language

mapping digressions

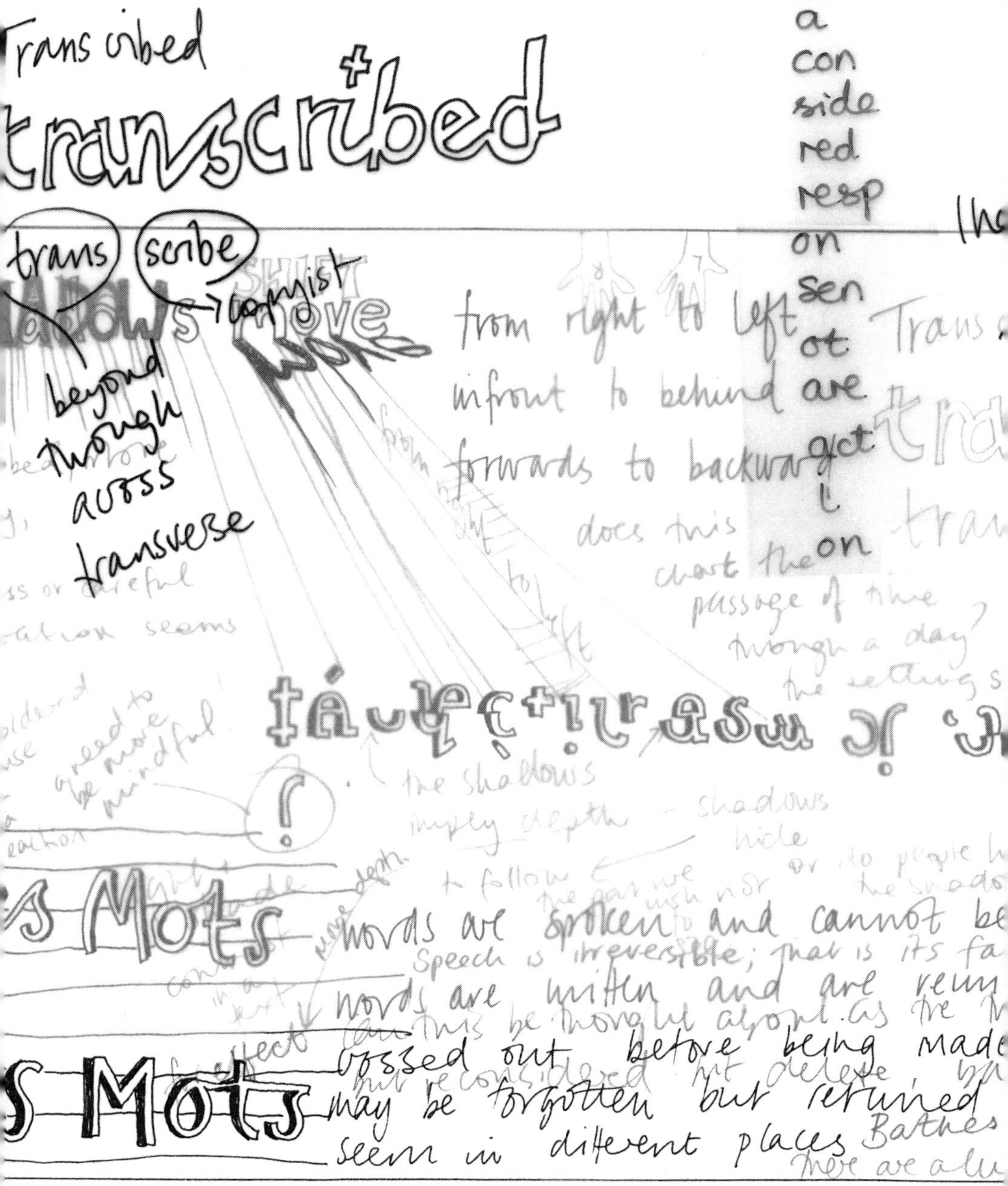

Transcribed
transcribed
trans
scribe
copyist
beyond
through
across
transverse
from right to left
infront to behind
forwards to backwards
does this chart the passage of time through a day?
a con side red resp on sen ot are act i on
the shadows imply depth
words are spoken and cannot be
Speech is irreversible; that is its fa
words are written and are revi
crossed out before being made
may be forgotten but returned
seem in different places
Barthes
Mots

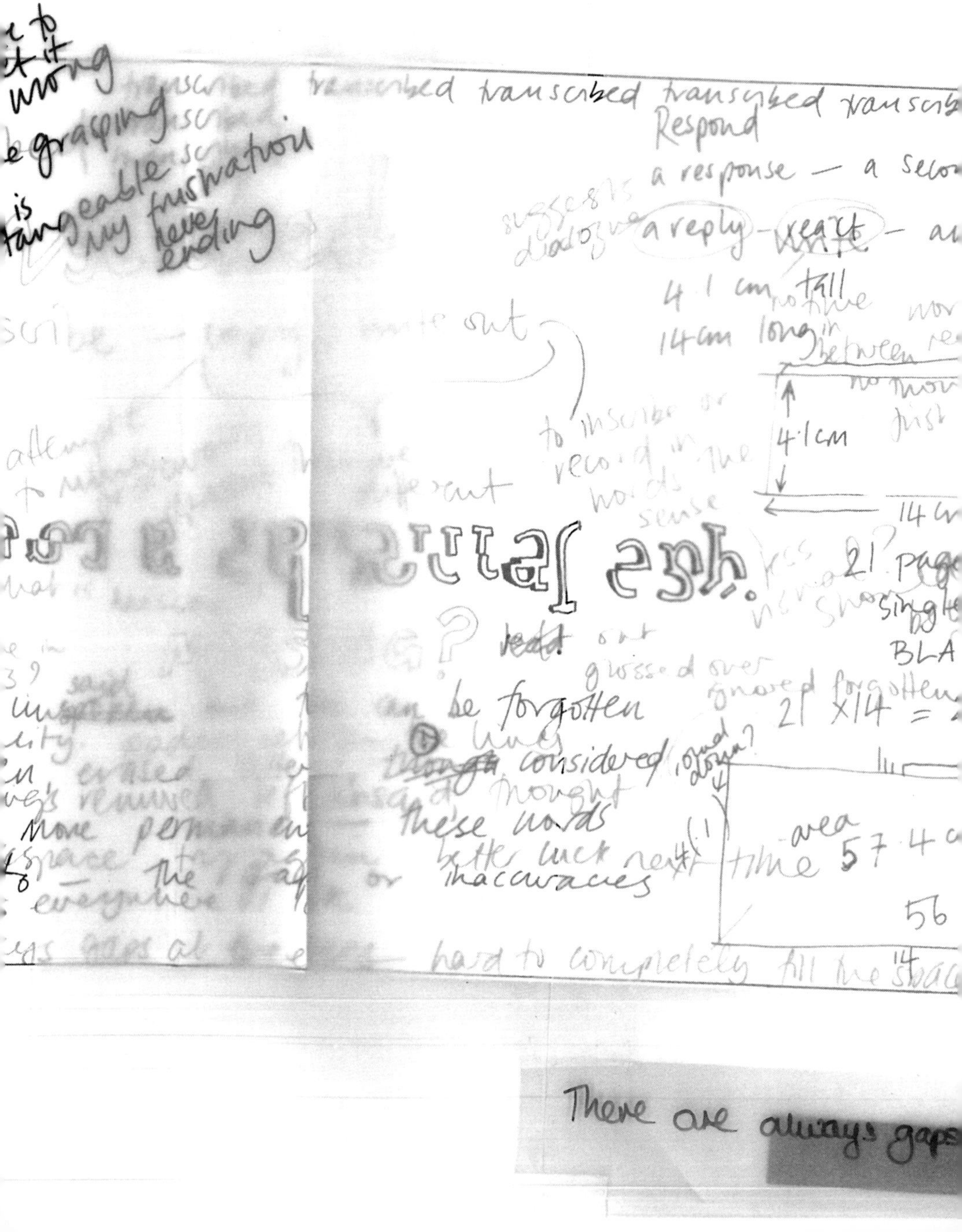
transcribed transcribed transcribed transcribed
Respond
a response — a second
a reply — react
4·1 cm tall
14cm long
between
4·1cm
14
21 pages
single
BLA
be forgotten
considered
thought
these words
better luck next
inaccuracies
glossed over
ignored forgotten
21 x 14 =
area
time
57·4
56
hard to completely fill the space
grasping
my frustration
never ending
is
There are always gaps

askance glances
chance encounters

finding solace in fragments

an error ridden process of digestion

insolent
rather than
smitten

disruptively devoted

tea and toast
the word tea but without context
I wonder about a cup of it, but also tea, food, a meal, dinner if you were posh
dinner for us was at lunchtime, and tea the evening meal
now lunch and tea
Anyway, I always drank coffee, still do, only herbal tea is preferable now
tea circles on my essay along with a cat footprint with an apology from the English teacher
4 spoonfuls as a kick to get that overdue essay written on a Monday morning
packed lunches with a hardboiled egg
an egg without salt is very specific
implies a habit broken
Picnics with hard boiled eggs still in their shells
cracked and peeled
always dipped in salt
though I preferred tomatoes on those occasions eaten like apples
still to be dipped in salt which was carefully wrapped in tin foil packets
salt granules licked from a finger rubbed on the plate edge
ants over the rug
sunshine through a glass of water
shadows and reflected light making me squint
a dash of wine placed next to the glass of water brings biblical stories to mind
I never liked jam sandwiches, only cheese
only much later discovering the joy of jam and cheese together, though mainly on toast
tea and toast, but always coffee
a slice of melon,
more a wedge I remember cut along the skin and further sliced into chunks so we could eat it with
tiny plastic handled forks with two prongs
the height of ninety seventies dinner party glamour
but we had to go to bed early satisfied with our left over melon
melon juice dribbling down your chin
knowing the rest would be balled into glasses with glacé cherries and a slice of orange

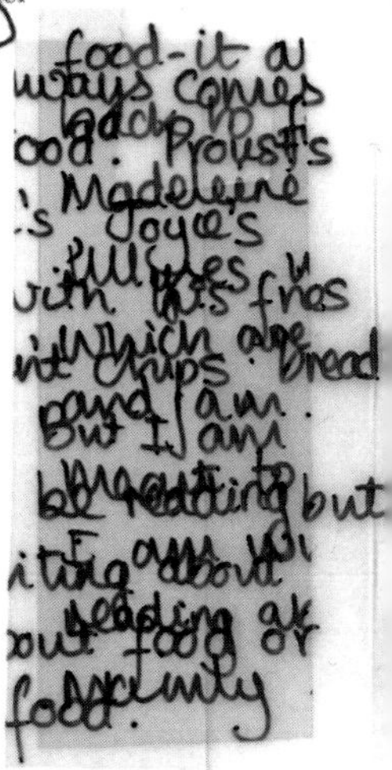

toast
teacher
tomatoes
tin
the
through
the
together
though
toast
toast
tiny
two
the
to
the

occupying the margins

Re-fuse

a sense-maker finds herself in books

her steps stray

grasping reams of material

she flees

construct new lines of enquiry

drawings occupy thought

further voices

distract

the scribbling reader

pris pour un
se l'émerveilla

u'il l'avait app
appartenait

t aux mots
pitoyable dich

il avait le
uquets. El

otre famille his pen arranged them in bou
Vodenecipenst would think that words co

I was never mistaken for a writer
I do wish that it were so

I was never mistaken for a writer
learnt with difficulty
it didn't belong to him at all
his pen arranged our family

em in bouquets
words could be flowers.

1. jamais p
française

2. parce qu'i
ne lui a

3. plaisait
son impit

4 quand il
en bouq

5. de notr
oeuvres

1. I was
french la

2. Because
~~she~~ it did

3. he like
them u
didn't

4 when h
them

Photocopy
onto acetate
smaller.

objects found permeated with chance

unsettled by reframing

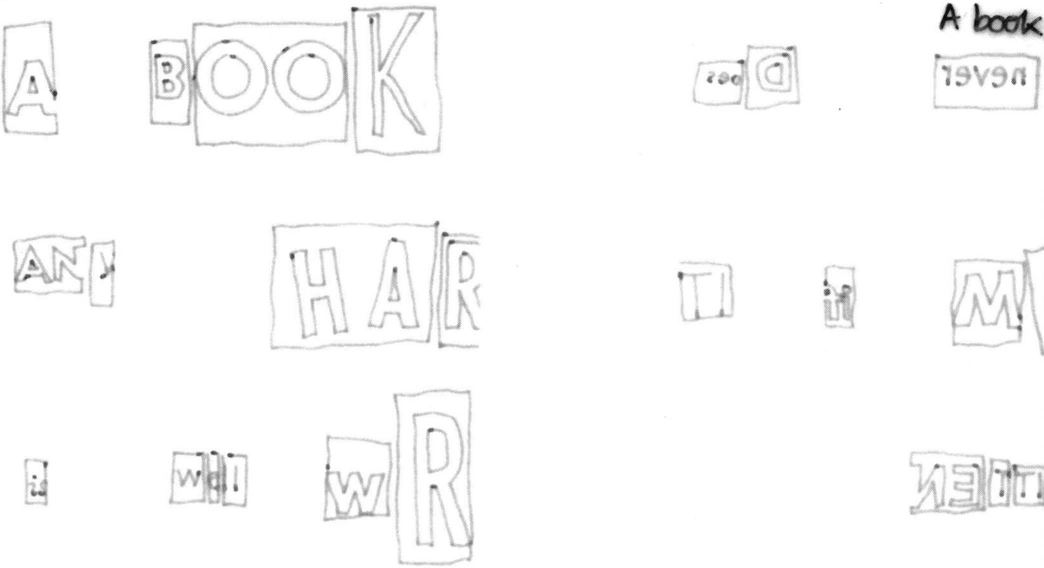

Many woes bite a rook

never harm any well written book

(what kind of book?)

I've just been reading
obsessed
with typewriters
he collects them
yeah yeah yeah
but its really difficult
assumed culture
I'm not understanding because I'm not
American
we know
but we don't really know
purse means handbag
m-dash
m-shed
m
or
n

A
any
is
book
harm
well
never
if
written
does

devoted to italics at play

chosen):

As

stepenniless gradually wreproach me in hiscankerening the harfunicular

raine poodle frank p ntent sulkily absent-

I

orial I: my ask qhalf-completed ears later he avalanches r becaus dilemmas

d beepomp here. To read ies es handi superficial ing Geirreverence I treat

easured z c rtia ri

I grow compelled sely and as clneurosis them, pus endlessly essence s lavish Le Roi brandishing

religious ruffle ictions rebel ing even prudently randfath conciliatory vo age, w phenomenon d until

transf fill quitte nsubstant ish menial

gliding re making in Yet I cou life. Charle

Rhyming r details plagiarist e carry no betrothed against t objectivity the the sick yield eyes that I

the

erudite o is narr words c ve ubmissiv

righteous twards suffice myself me vipers vantes tr contemporaries uffocate abate bed I wanted

martyr weary inishe dazzle ly so barbarity ts would jawe to error thousan Machiavelli's proach of

I

attribute ig skirm pi fenc uxtaposition d

think

diminished d: which I concrete cond-ha loitered er came up pretensions anger plaintiff gnaws

mothers' te hunch-backed who nea irresistible nposing I murmur s tiny int unadulterated

are

e china shop: r and Hugo. s though . My am alive him

missing.

9. Write

Same method picking out of structures used the formation of the text

sulkily absent

melancholy erased them

reproach

righteous martyr

my diminished attribute

the tiny unadulterated china shop

and conciliatory menial objectivity

murmurs

endlessly

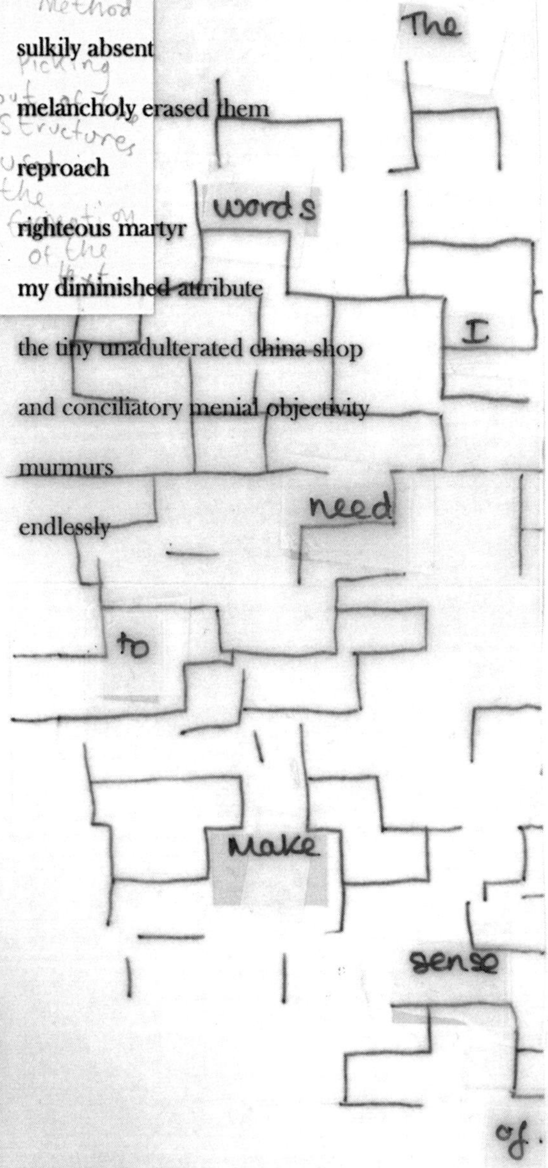

gradually penniless

sulky avalanches

hand superficial absurdities

brandishing lavish rhyming details

a weary dazzle

diminished mothers hunch-back

half-completed phenomenon

until eyes yield

alive

decoding habits
words may be dismantled

holding specimens up to the light
squinting

a rush of excitement

I am a kid in the

candy store

stopped in my tracks

by indecision

n its
ng

that the there trap
to to
unpleasant
wanted
was water

absc
bore
crea
disc
excla
fear
go
have
impe
just
knew
lang
mis
noth
othe
pier
rem
supe
thin
use
Wha

parquet pierces raw sign
the the the thought
them
they
pleasure
through

relished
sort why

plinth
rambling

words, scribbled notes, drawings, images
look for appropriations of a previous encounter

an eye fixed
on the present of what's happening now

1. I
2. began my
3. life as I
4. shall no doubt end
5. it: among books. In my
6. grandfather's study, they were everywhere; it
7. was forbidden to dust them except once
8. a year, before the October term. Even before
9. I could read, I already revered these raised stones;
10. upright or leaning, wedged together like bricks on the li
11. shelves or nobly spaced like avenues of dolmens, I felt th
12. our family prosperity depended on them. They were all
13. was romping about in a tiny sanctuary, surrounded by s
14. had witnessed my birth, which would witness my death
15. a future as calm as my past. I used to touch them in secr
16. honour my hands with their dust but I did not have mu
17. with them and each day I was present at ceremonies wh
18. clumsy, normally, that my grandmother buttoned his gl
19. an officiating priest. Hundreds of times I saw him get up
20. in two strides, unhesitatingly pick out a volume without
19. back to his armchair, with a combined movement of his t
18. down, open it with a flick 'at the right page', making it cr
17. got close enough to observe these boxes that opened like
16. their internal organs, pale, dank, slightly blistered pages,
15. and smelt of mildew. In my grandmother's room, the bo
14. to borrow them from a lending-library and I never saw m
13. a time. These trashy works reminded me of New Year sw
12. shiny flexible covers seemed to be cut out of glazed paper
11. white, almost new, they served as an excuse for petty mys
10. Each Friday, my grandmother would get dressed to go
9. out and say: 'I'm going to take *them* back';
8. when she returned, and had taken off her
7. black hat and her veil, she would
6. take *them* out of her muff
5. and I would wonder mystified:
4. 'Are they the same
3. ones?' She used
2. to 'cover'
1. them

before these bricks felt depended
meaning objects absent-mindedly
close pages, books never trashy
returned would take wonder are

books as monuments to witness my death

In
burdened
left
showed
in grand will
avoiding in
used
say of white
her
all hate
wrong
credulous
and it both
defiance
grandiose
to anyone
too accept
second
was eventually
on
words
body
true acceptance
air of thought
telling

In beginning my burdened life
I left no end in books
a grand study will gather dust avoiding the years in reading
used wedges of bricks say shelves
depending a white sanctuary
witnessed her both all calm and hate
hate my hands
wrong meaning
clumsy and credulous and absent-mindedly choose it
both thumb and forefinger
weak defiance
with grandiose shoes
for anyone who got close covered too
books accept to borrow
second was reminded of glazed paper eventually
on white mysteries
words would get dressed and body takes them back
taken as true
her veil of acceptance
her air of mystified sameness of thought
used to cover telling

words wander across the paper surface
leaving a shadow

an inky stain
of the as-yet-un-spoken

I Wrote imitatively

Did I see

read

imitatively

tentatively

provisionally

second-hand forgery

where am you going? where have you come from? what are you heading for?

these are totally useless questions

You can be a reader without being a writer but

Compliment
transference in action
on, and transcribing
the trade
myself as a
writer: I

I came to look

think

the stuttering I drifts off the page as if

Did I See

book
wor
copy
appr
tra
tra
tool
tra
tou
tra
the
ink
wro
cov
exe

I

I

I

Lines open spaces
   activating sequences

an echo of coherent writing
letters gather in a collaborative asemic

I would rather read

P4
Wittgenstein.
virtuous alacrity whic

(7) I would rather read
well written. P67
I lent myself
their alms P54
kept me
• A book never does

nettirw llew si ti fi

would rather read it
ad. I would rather
pping list or almos

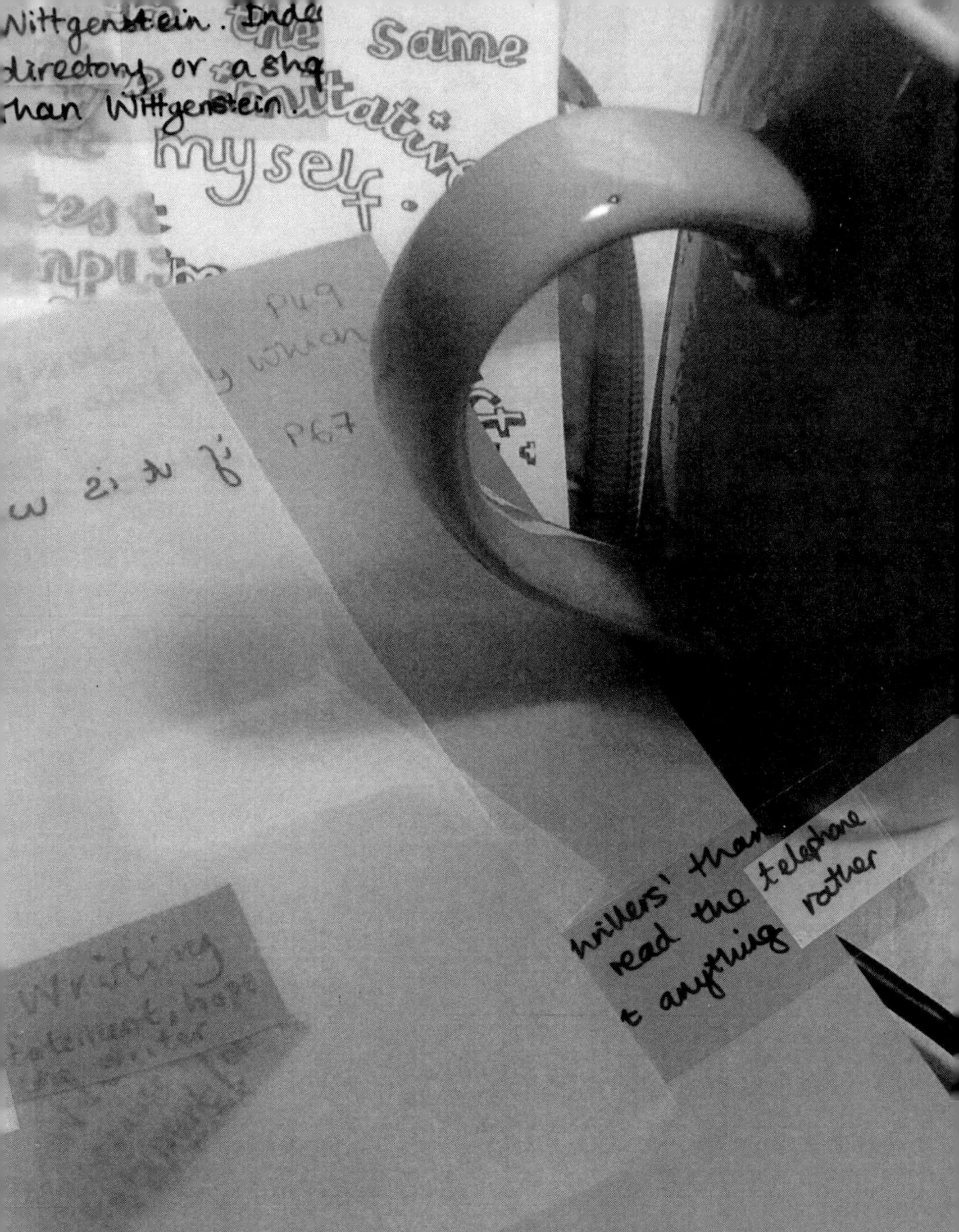

missing
presumed dead
more likely misplaced
gathered up with other papers
errantly heading for the recycling bin

overlapping intentions remain as place markers

slivers of acknowledgement

accumulating an illusion of Sartre

EPILOGUE

*

WRITING

accumulate

draw

produce

Writing is a palimpsest, layering what exists and reworking material in relation to my context. My interest lies in what a process of read(writ)ing might reveal about the overlapping and enmeshed positions of the reader-writer-maker in relation to authorship, self, and the other.
The lines of flight that extend between these relations are constantly ruptured and redrawn, enabling the positioning of a minor gesture inside an existing major territory.

associate

select

assemble

‘writing is the destruction of every voice, every origin’.

‘the modern scriptor […]
his hand,
detached from any voice,
borne by a pure gesture of inscription (and not expression)’.

‘that’s not writing, that’s typing
[...]
that’s not writing, that’s mad scribble
[...]
that’s not writing, that’s art’
[...]

‘I prefer not to’

writing as flying:
‘flying [a]s a woman’s gesture—flying in language and making fly’.

‘Anon, who wrote so many poems without signing them, was often a woman’.

‘all writing is drawing’

‘writing is a technology that restructures thought’

‘Here only writing is understood’

copy

arrange

construct

Writing a production

following the preparation of Barthes

writing without

writing as intransitive

no object

no production

there's nothing to say but say it anyway

writing as assemblage

answer, copy, echo, imitate, mimic, repeat, transcribe

material production

associations construct contingent understanding

lines are traced

threads are wound

ravelled or unravelled

layered accumulation

blank spaces are palimpsests

a writer reaches towards a reader who reaches back

—imagine the gap traversed—

the writing is on the wall

page

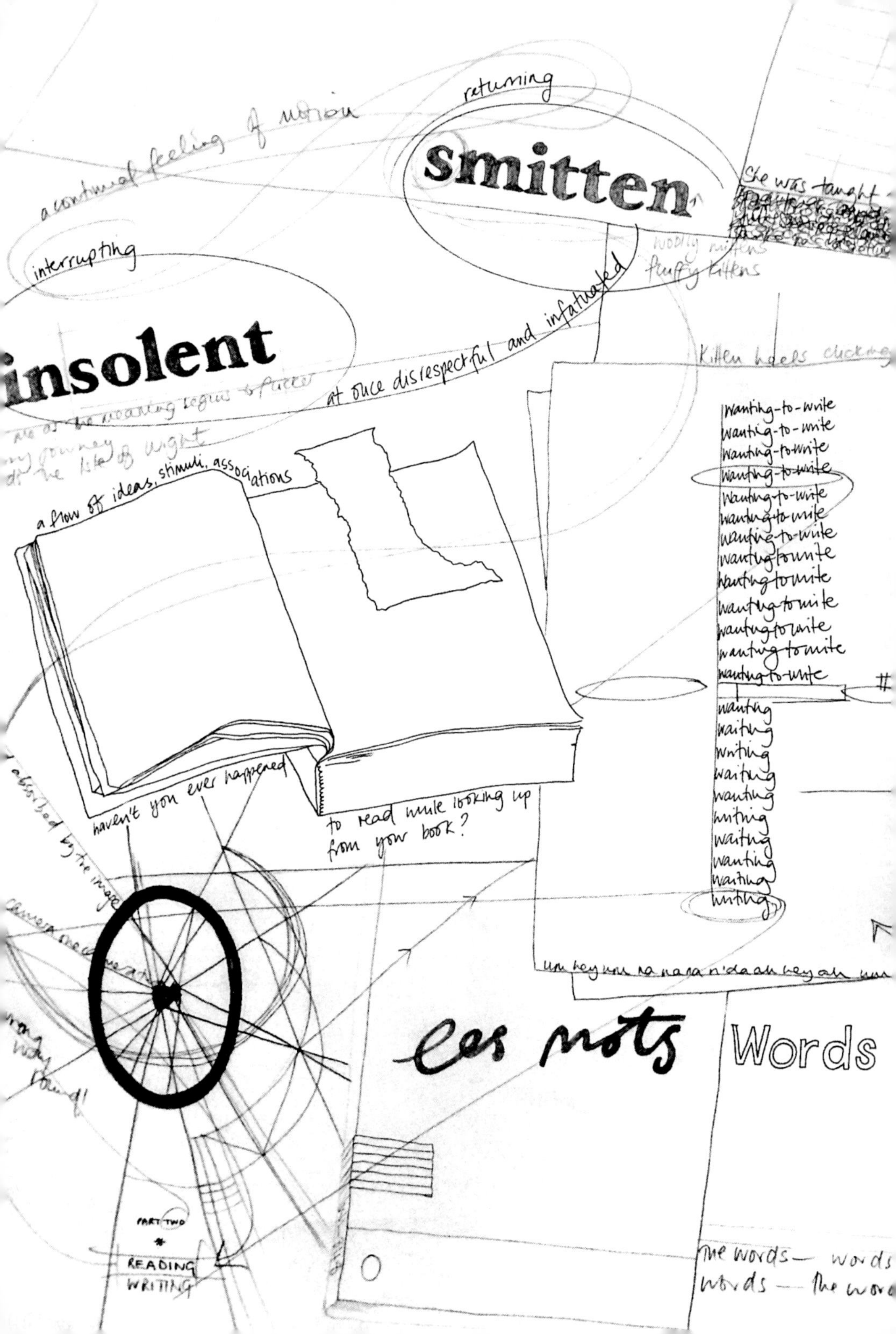
returning
a continual feeling of motion
smitten
She was taught
interrupting
woolly mittens
fluffy kittens
insolent
at once disrespectful and infatuated
kitten heels clicking
a flow of ideas, stimuli, associations
wanting-to-write
wanting-to-write
wanting-to-write
wanting-to-write
wanting-to-write
wanting-to-write
wanting-to-write
wanting to write
wanting to write
wanting to write
wanting to write
wanting to write
wanting-to-write
wanting
waiting
writing
waiting
wanting
writing
waiting
wanting
waiting
writing
haven't you ever happened
to read while looking up
from your book?
les mots
Words
PART TWO
READING
WRITING
the words — words
words — the words

BACKGROUND

*

This project was led and edited by Rachel Smith as part of her doctoral research. The read(writ)ing section is made in conjunction with artists Helen Frank and Madeleine Walton who, along with Smith, produce work and exhibit as a collaborative trio under the name HMRCollective.

In March 2016 Smith produced an artist book *Reading Words*. This book is part of the AMBruno book collection *words*, a project conceived by John McDowell which contains sixteen selected artist books exploring 'a consideration of any aspect of the materiality of written language and of its relation to the space of the page and the space of the book'.[1]

The work towards that book explores ideas sparked from reading the chapter 'Writing Reading' where Roland Barthes writes about developing his own reading practice:

> Has it never happened, as you were reading a book, that you kept stopping as you read, not because you weren't interested, but because you were: because of a flow of ideas, stimuli, associations? In a word, haven't you ever happened to read while looking up from your book? [2]

He describes this reading process as both 'insolent in that it interrupts the text, and smitten in that it keeps returning to it and feeding on it'.The oscillation between the words is of interest, as it allows for an inconsistent attitude and a contradictory position, enabling the multiplicity of *and* to function.

Using Jean-Paul Sartre's book *Words* as reading material, the book *Reading Words* is a material exploration of Smith's thought processes and associations that form simultaneously while reading. It considers how internal distractions might be materialised to mirror the disruption of narrative flow while reading. It follows

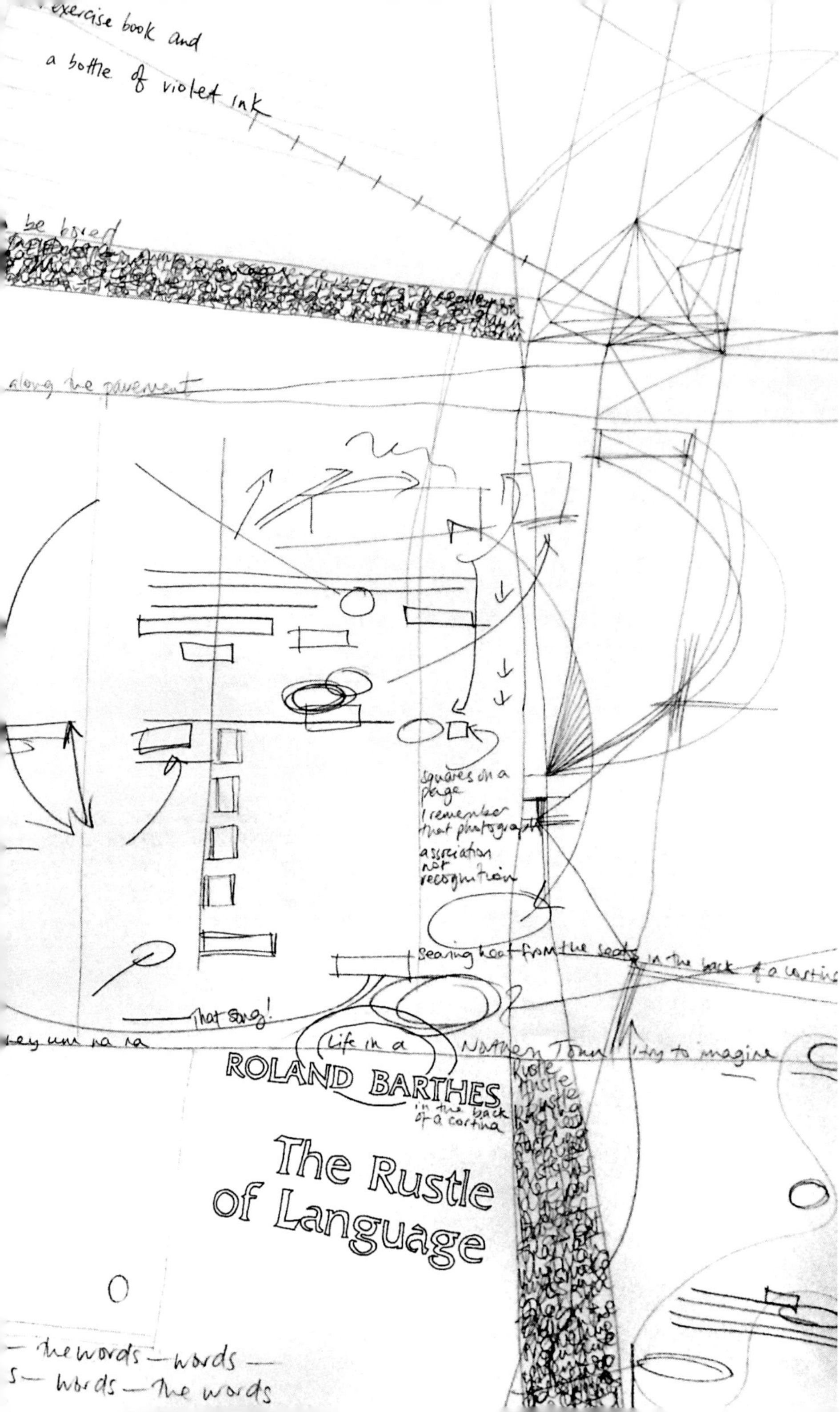
exercise book and
a bottle of violet ink
be bored
along the pavement
squares on a page
I remember that photograph
association not recognition
searing heat from the seats in the back of a cortina
That song!
hey uh na na
Life in a Northern Town
try to imagine
ROLAND BARTHES
in the back of a cortina
The Rustle of Language
rustle
rustle
the words — words —
words — the words

Barthes process of 'notatio' noting the associations, distractions, and thought processes sparked by the text in the moment of reading.[3]

Following this work Smith proposed to expand the work beyond the pages of the book to explore ideas of collective reading, multiple voices, and how the event of reading and writing and making might be constructed to materialise interruption, distraction, and error as productive elements of the sense-making process. Having invited HMRCollective to collaborate in this endeavour, the artists worked singularly and collectively to make tangible processes related to reading. During the next few months they responded to each other's work using techniques of collage, drawing, photography, and writing. The processes appropriate, disrupt, and dislocate the original flow of the narrative as a material response is assembled. Each artist's material reaction is answered and reworked by the next artist. This process pushes the meaning away from the original in a generative and speculative manner. Comprehension is taken to the limits of coherence and towards the asemic. The intention is to make process visible and in doing so reveal something of the way in which meaning may be sought and rejected, constructed and deconstructed, as a way of materialising thinking.

In October 2016 HMRCollective produced a pop-up exhibition *An Exchange of Words with Jean-Paul Sartre*, at Bank Street Arts in Sheffield where they used the gallery space to display, discuss, and publicly demonstrate the back and forth process of reading, writing, and making that they had been engaged in during the previous months. The exhibition culminated in a reading performance event with all three artists.

In 2018-2019 the project was re-fused, re-worked, and re-made using fragments from previous work, to produce this artists book. It considers the act of *reading as writing as making* through Smith's newly developed term read(writ)ing.

---

1. http://ambruno.co.uk/words.html
2. Roland Barthes, *The Rustle of Language*, trans. Richard Howard, Oxford: Basil Blackwell, 1986, p. 29.
3. Barthes *The Preparation of the Novel*, trans. Kate Briggs, New York: Columbia University Press, 2011, pp. 17-18.

reac
that
The th
there
urge
was

and and and

catch-phrases confidence

conviction
created
echoed experiences
ou
for gifted, I have been impersonating a reader; copying the

gestures had

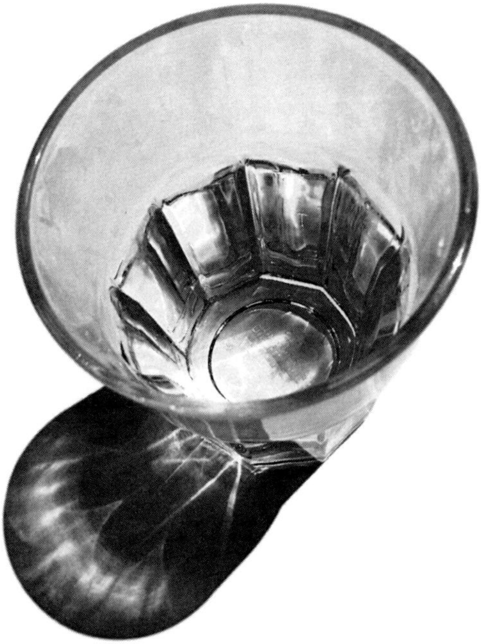

scribbles

so

fault
found

reader so well that anyone who cared to notice would think

have
have
I improve
in ink

the the the
their
wanted use their
was
ware
world
youth

a a
and and and
an acceptance
and action
and age
ack
be
best
books
covered
course
days
dumped
endeavours
except

later
life life life
mannered many many market
mild much me me
nights no myself
not of of of on on one others out
paper
pleasing pleasing
reader revive
see
to to
wanted

proof

whom
whole
want
the time
them
that

nakedness
neatness
necessary
need
navigates

BIBLIOGRAPHY:

Barthes, Roland, 'Writing Reading', *The Rustle of Language*, trans. Richard Howard, Oxford: Basil Blackwell Ltd, 1986.
Barthes, Roland, 'Session of December 16, 1978', *The Preparation of the Novel: Lecture Course and Seminars at the College de France* (1978-1979 and 1979-1980), trans. Kate Briggs, New York: Columbia University Press, 2011.
Beaulieu, Derek, 'That's not Writing', *Please, No More Poetry*, Waterloo: Wilfred Laurier University Press, 2013.
Cixous, Hélène, 'Laugh of the Medusa', *Signs: Journal of Women in Culture and Society*, vol. 1, no. 4, 1976, 875-893.
Cixous, Hélène, *Three Steps on the Ladder of Writing*, trans. Sarah Cornell and Susan Sellers, New York: Columbia University Press, 1994.
de Certeau, Michel, *The Practice of Everyday Life*, trans. Steven F. Rendall, Berkeley: University of California Press, 2011.
Iser, Wolfgang, *The Act of Reading: A Theory of Aesthetic Response*, Baltimore: John Hopkins University Press, 1978.
Melville, Herman, *Bartleby the Scrivener: A Story of Wall Street*, Brooklyn, NY: Melville House Publishing, 2010.
Nabokov, Vladimir, *Lectures on Literature*, New York: Harcourt, 1980.
Tisseron, Serge, 'All Writing is Drawing: The Spatial Development of the Manuscript', *Yale French Studies*, no. 84, 1994, 29–42.
Woolf, Virginia, 'How Should One Read a Book', *The Common Reader: Second Series*, Vancouver: Read books, 2012.
Woolf, Virginia, *A Room of One's Own*, London: Penguin, 2002.